The Duke of Lancaster's Own Yeomanry

A short history
compiled from regimental and other records

by Fergus Read

Lancashire County Books
1992

The Duke of Lancaster's Own Yeomanry
A short history compiled from regimental and other records

by Fergus Read

Copyright © Lancashire County Books, 1992

Text copyright © Fergus Read, 1992

First edition, 1992

Designed and typeset in 10½/12 Times by Carnegie Publishing Ltd., Preston
Printed and bound by The Bath Press, Bath.

British Library Cataloguing-in-Publication Data
A CIP catalogue record for this book is available from the British Library

ISBN 0-871236-11-8

Contents

Preface

THIS work by its very length cannot tell the full history of the Regiment. It should be read in conjunction with the history *Trumpet Call* by Desmond Bastick, which it aims to supplement rather than supersede. Together these works must serve until a full history can be produced. For the specialist areas of uniforms, a recent work by Smith and Barlow (see bibliography) can also be highly recommended.

The author is aware that there are many omissions in this work – in particular that most personal names have been left out. This is a deliberate move, in recognition that it would be invidious to mention some and not others in so short a work. The author would welcome information regarding inaccuracies in the text, which will be corrected in future editions.

The museum of the Regiment is housed within the Lancashire County and Regimental Museum on Stanley Street, Preston. The collection is cared for as a loan by the Lancashire County Museum Service. The author was formerly Keeper of Military History for the Museum Service.

Acknowledgements

THE author would like to thank Mark Abbott, Bob Dobson, Philip Mather and Bill Turner for giving useful research leads, while the reference librarians at Blackpool, Bolton, Lancaster, Liverpool, Manchester, Preston, Rochdale and Southport have assisted in many ways. The majority of the illustrations are from the Regimental collection, and thanks are due to the Regimental Museum Trustees for permission to reproduce them. The following also kindly gave permission to use illustrative material:

John Anderson
B. Walker
Illustrated London News
Bolton Library Archives
Lancaster City Museums
Ministry of Defence
Bernard Walker

The History of the Duke of Lancaster's Own Yeomanry

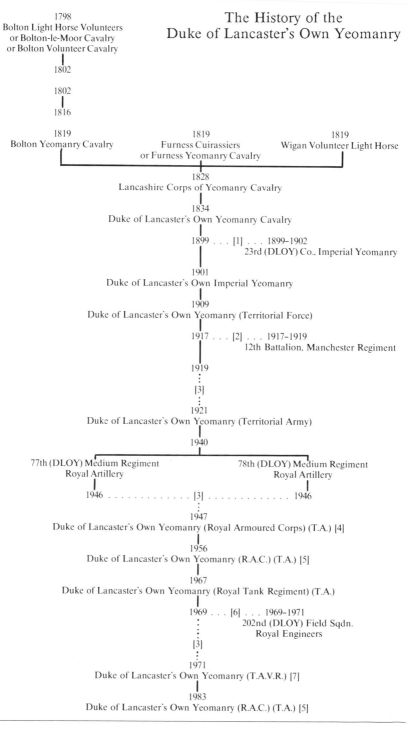

1798
Bolton Light Horse Volunteers
or Bolton-le-Moor Cavalry
or Bolton Volunteer Cavalry

1802

1802

1816

1819
Bolton Yeomanry Cavalry

1819
Furness Cuirassiers
or Furness Yeomanry Cavalry

1819
Wigan Volunteer Light Horse

1828
Lancashire Corps of Yeomanry Cavalry

1834
Duke of Lancaster's Own Yeomanry Cavalry

1899 . . . [1] . . . 1899–1902
23rd (DLOY) Co., Imperial Yeomanry

1901
Duke of Lancaster's Own Imperial Yeomanry

1909
Duke of Lancaster's Own Yeomanry (Territorial Force)

1917 . . . [2] . . . 1917–1919
12th Battalion, Manchester Regiment

1919

[3]

1921
Duke of Lancaster's Own Yeomanry (Territorial Army)

1940

77th (DLOY) Medium Regiment
Royal Artillery

78th (DLOY) Medium Regiment
Royal Artillery

1946 . . . . [3] 1946

1947
Duke of Lancaster's Own Yeomanry (Royal Armoured Corps) (T.A.) [4]

1956
Duke of Lancaster's Own Yeomanry (R.A.C.) (T.A.) [5]

1967
Duke of Lancaster's Own Yeomanry (Royal Tank Regiment) (T.A.)

1969 . . . [6] . . . 1969–1971
202nd (DLOY) Field Sqdn.
Royal Engineers

[3]

1971
Duke of Lancaster's Own Yeomanry (T.A.V.R.) [7]

1983
Duke of Lancaster's Own Yeomanry (R.A.C.) (T.A.) [5]

---

[1] 102 officers and men volunteer as mounted infantry
[2] 132 officers and men drafted as infantry
[3] Reduced to a cadre
[4] Role as Divisional Armoured Regiment
[5] Role as Home Defence Reconnaissance Regiment
[6] Transfer of name only
[7] Role as Infantry Home Defence Regiment.

Chapter One

Origins of the Regiment
1798–1834

A Need for Volunteers

*T*he origins of the Duke of Lancaster's Own Yeomanry can be traced to the end of the eighteenth century, when Britain was at war with Revolutionary France, and invasion seemed to threaten. The Volunteer Act of 1794 was the first of many Acts of Parliament intended to encourage men to 'voluntarily enrol themselves for the Defence of their counties, towns and coasts, or for the General Defence of the Kingdom, during the present war'. Both infantry and cavalry units were raised, the latter often being known as 'Gentlemen and Yeomanry Cavalry', in time shortened to 'Yeomanry'.

Lancashire Cavalry Volunteers

*T*he records of the yeomanry units raised in Lancashire during the French wars are scant; some were short-lived, and many changed their titles, or used them inconsistently. To add further to the confusion most of the volunteer units in Britain disbanded in 1802 following the Peace of Amiens, only to be revived, not always under the same officers, as the Peace broke down.

The following volunteer cavalry units were in existence in 1804, near the height of the invasion scare. They appear in *A list of the Officers of the Gentlemen and Yeomanry Cavalry and Volunteer Infantry of the United Kingdom* published by the War Office in October, 1804:

Ashton Cavalry – Captain William Gerard, Bt.
Bolton-le-Moor Cavalry – Major John Pilkington
Liverpool Light Horse – Major Edward Faulkner[1]
Manchester & Salford Light Horse – Major Shakespear Philips

The modern regiment that is the subject of this history, the Duke of Lancaster's Own Yeomanry, can claim a descent from the Bolton unit, which was raised in 1798, following the exertions of a well-known Bolton business figure, John Pilkington, variously described as a 'manufacturer' and 'builder', and who became the unit's first 'commandant'. It should be noted that at other times during the Revolutionary and Napoleonic Wars volunteer cavalry units are also recorded as existing in Oldham, Blackburn, Bury, Preston and Chorley.[2]

The Early Recruits

O *fficer's Commissions* in each unit were granted on the King's authority by the County Lords Lieutenant, and were generally held by the landowning nobility and gentry, the ranks being filled by yeomen and tenant farmers. All had to provide their own horse, hence the agricultural bias, but saddlery and uniforms were usually paid for by the officers or by subscriptions raised in the counties.[3] Swords and pistols were provided by the government.

Training Commitments

T *he* Lancashire units of volunteer cavalry were invariably committed to serve throughout the county as required. At a time of invasion they were liable to defend the wider Northern Military District, and some voted (democracy was a feature of some units, at least in the early days) to make themselves available for service anywhere in the country. Volunteers undertook to make themselves available for drill on two days each week, totalling a minimum of six hours, and also to attend an annual full-time training, or 'permanent duty', which could last several weeks. Training was usually paid, at a rate similar to regular cavalry, and non-attenders could be fined. This was the theory.

However, the reality at this time was that the commanding officers determined the frequency of parades and the disciplining of non-attenders. After initial enthusiasm, and especially after the threat of invasion had passed, many units held only irregular parades, and reduced the length of their annual 'permanent duty' to the minimum eight days, also choosing to include as part of this the time that it took to ride to the training grounds. Such arrangements suited both officer and ranker who, being often landowner and tenant respectively, shared a concern that their military duties should not interfere with their work on the land. In later years the requirement for training was more closely regulated, with the annual camps (as they became known) culminating in an inspection by a high ranking officer of the regular cavalry, who would designate the unit 'efficient' or otherwise. Continued government support might rest on that report. However, the timing of the yeomanry annual camps was always determined, until well into this century, by the need to avoid busy times of the farm year. The end of June was the norm across the country, although the weather could alter this. During permanent duty the volunteers could be billeted and disciplined like regulars.

Avoidance and Tax and Militia

*R*ecruitment was undoubtedly helped by the exemption from various new war taxes granted to members, such as horse duty and hair powder tax. Volunteers up to 1808 were also excused the militia ballot, an important consideration for men of yeoman status. The militia by the end of the eighteenth century was little more than a form of emergency conscripted service for those unable to avoid it. Since Tudor times each county had been required to raise a quota of men liable for duty in a county militia in times of crisis. Registers of all able-bodied men were maintained and ballots held to determine who was to serve. Substitutes could be provided but they had to be paid by the individuals for whom they were standing substitute. The militia ranks as a result usually contained a high proportion of society misfits. Moreover during the French wars the militia regiments were embodied almost continuously for permanent duty, causing obvious problems to a yeoman farmer, if not to the landless farm labourer.

The Lancashire yeomanry units varied greatly in size, both in themselves and compared with each other, although evidence can only be gleaned for isolated years. The 'Bolton Cavalry' were authorised in 1798 to raise two troops, approximately a hundred men, and the earliest surviving roll appears to confirm that they achieved this: John Pilkington is recorded in the *Returns: Volunteers of the United Kingdom*, corrected to 1804, as commanding a force of 116, composed of one field officer, two subalterns, three staff officers, six sergeants, two trumpeters and one hundred rank and file. However, two years later James Wilson's *A View of the Volunteer Army of the United Kingdom* (1806) gave the strength as being only 65. It would appear that support for the yeomanry had waned, perhaps, one might think, a result of the naval victory at Trafalgar in October 1805, which had all but removed the threat of invasion. But even before Trafalgar the support was perhaps slipping in Bolton. A muster roll for a parade and inspection at Preston in June 1805 lists 86 names (an acceptable shortfall on the authorised strength for two troops, given a normal

---

To the EDITOR *of the* MANCHESTER OBSERVER.

SIR,—It perhaps may not be uninteresting to the patriotic portion of your readers to know that the Bolton Loyal Troop of Yeomanry Cavalry have mustered regularly for the last five days, for the sole and only purpose of legalizing their exemption from the Horse Duty, which would have become due on the 5th of the present month. Two or three of the days were uncommonly wet; however, they mounted for a few minutes, and then dismissed, through which redoubtable service, the revenue will be minus in this district above 300*l.* This notable fact puts the Reformers in a similar situation to that of Plutarch's Wolf, who, peeping into a hut beheld a company of shepherds regaling themselves over a joint of mutton. Lord! said he, what a clamour these men would have raised, if they had caught me at such a banquet.

I am, Sir, yours, &c.

A FRIEND TO TRUTH.

Bolton, April 3, 1820.

Letter as printed in the *Manchester Observer* in April 1820, accusing the Bolton Yeomanry of mustering merely to claim exemption from the horse tax.

turnover in recruits) but nearly a quarter of these are marked as 'absent', albeit mostly 'with leave', including the Captain, Cornet, Chaplain and Surgeon.[4] Such generous leave-taking lends weight to the charge often levied at the time that the yeomanry existed more to enable privileged members to avoid taxation and the militia ballot, than to present any credible military force.

Popular criticism of the yeomanry was not, however, limited to tax evasion, shirking and inefficiency; as the invasion threat declined the continued existence of yeomanry forces was interpreted as a political act. Certainly official interest in the yeomanry was not confined to times of military threat. From the start they had also been widely used by the County Lords Lieutenant in a policing role and in fact throughout the first half of the nineteenth century the yeomanry were used as an armed security force, as were the regular troops and militia, in the absence of a formal police force.[5] The Volunteer Act of 1804, which consolidated and amended the previous Acts relating to Volunteers, refers specifically to situations of 'rebellion' and 'riot' when considering the rules governing the emergency use of yeomanry. As men of property themselves, the yeomanry readily responded to counter any incident that was seen as a threat to social order, be it machine breaking, election riots, or reform and protest meetings.

Luddites

*M*ost serious at this time were fears among textile workers that the widespread use of powered machines would lead to reduced wages and high unemployment. This led to a spate of machine breaking attacks, especially in factories in the Nottinghamshire lace and Yorkshire woollen areas. Machine-breakers, or 'Luddites' (so named after the fictitious 'General Ludd' whose signature was on many of their slogans), were particularly active in 1812. In Lancashire, mills at Middleton and Westhoughton were attacked. Bolton magistrate 'Colonel' Ralph Fletcher feared that the widespread attacks were co-ordinated and part of a general conspiracy in the country.

He went so far as to employ spies among the workpeople in Lancashire. His efforts did not prevent serious damage to Wroe and Duncough's Mill at Westhoughton, although the Bolton Light Horse did round up some of those thought to be involved, three of whom (including a thirteen-year-old boy) were later hanged as ringleaders after a trial at Lancaster. Major Pilkington, commander (and, of course, founder) of the Bolton Light Horse, together with Major Buller of the Royal Scots Greys (a regular cavalry regiment), were presented with gold snuff boxes after the disturbances, as a 'memorial of public gratitude for their prompt and judicious exertions during the late disturbances in the manufacturing districts in suppressing the riotous proceedings of misled and ignorant people'.[6]

New or revived units

Manchester and Salford Yeomanry Cavalry
Re-raised 1817.   Commanded by Major Thomas Joseph Trafford
(from 1820 by Major Hugh Hornby Birley).

Oldham Yeomanry Cavalry
Re-raised 1817.   Captain John Taylor.

*Bolton Yeomanry Cavalry
Re-raised 1919.   Captain James Kearsley.

*Furness Cuirassiers, or Furness Yeomanry Cavalry
Raised 1819.   Captain Thomas Richmond Gale Braddyll.

*Wigan Volunteer Light Horse
Raised 1819.   Captain John Hodson Kearsley.

Units which continued

Ashton Volunteer Cavalry, or Ashton Yeomanry Cavalry
Captain Sir William Gerard Bt.

Liverpool Light Horse Volunteers, or Liverpool Yeomanry Cavalry
Major Edward Falkner.

---

*   Units from which the current regiment can claim direct descent.

Post-war Depression

*T*he French wars finally ended in 1815 and most of the volunteer units that remained quickly disbanded. However, economic depression after the war led to tension in both agricultural and industrial areas, and the government was soon prepared to see yeomanry units revived and, indeed, new ones formed, to serve as an 'aid to the Civil Power'.

The government remained worried by the yeomanry's lack of organisation and training, and in 1816 new regulations provided for six days' paid training per year during peacetime, but only for yeomanry regiments of three or more troops; a clear attempt to encourage amalgamation. However, in Lancashire this had no effect – the Liverpool and Ashton Yeomanries were almost certainly smaller than this but retained a fierce independence, while the government itself sanctioned the formation of two new units (in Furness and Wigan) and the re-raising of two others (in Oldham and Bolton), each of which was only one troop (approximately fifty all ranks) strong. With continued civil unrest, the government let the matter rest.

The major discontent in Lancashire centred on the textile industry. The power-loom became widely used in Lancashire in the 1820s, and high unemployment among hand-loom weavers led to tension across the area. At Blackburn, Bacup, Bury, Clitheroe, Rawtenstall, Haslingden, Shaw and Oldham the weavers showed their frustration in a spate of power-loom breaking over several days at the end of April 1826. To disperse the rioters the Bolton and Oldham Yeomanry were called out, and probably other units, although records are lacking. Interestingly, a yeomanry unit from Craven, Yorkshire, is recorded as assembling at Clitheroe in Lancashire, troops from Lord Ribblesdale's Yeomanry, facing rioters at Low Moor until the 2nd Dragoon Guards (regular cavalry) arrived.[7]

Peterloo

*H*owever, the most famous incident to involve yeomanry in Lancashire in the immediate post-war period occurred in 1819 at St Peter's Fields, Manchester, and centred on demands for political reforms. A large crowd, variously estimated at between sixty and eighty thousand, gathered on 16 August to hear the Radical speaker Henry Hunt argue for the right to vote as a solution to the working people's economic plight. The local magistrates responded by calling out special constables and military assistance, which included the Manchester and Salford Yeomanry. This unit, re-raised in 1817 with two troops, was notable for finding its recruits not from agriculture but from an urban middle class of horse-owning tradesmen, especially cotton merchants and manufacturers, publicans and shopkeepers.[8]

Once the meeting started, although it was peaceful, the Deputy Constable of Manchester was instructed by the magistrates to arrest Hunt. The cavalry were ordered to force a way through the crowd for him, and the Manchester and Salford Yeomanry, about a hundred strong, moved first. An eyewitness described the scene:

At first their movement was not rapid, and there was some show of an attempt to follow their officer in regular succession, five or six abreast; but they soon increased their speed . . . seeming to vie individually with each other which should be first . . . As the cavalry approached the dense mass of people they used their utmost efforts to escape: but so closely were they pressed in opposite directions by the soldiers, the special constables, the position of the hustings, and their own immense numbers, that immediate escape was impossible . . . On their arrival at the hustings a scene of dreadful confusion ensued. The orators fell or were forced off the scaffold in quick succession; fortunately for them, the stage being rather elevated, they were in great degree beyond the reach of the many swords which gleamed around them.[9]

Hunt was thus arrested, offering no resistance, and the crowd was already trying to disperse. The yeomanry had seemed effective if clumsy. Several reports later claimed that some of the yeomanry

A hostile contemporary illustration depicting the Manchester & Salford Yeomanry striking out at the crowd at Peterloo.

appeared to be drunk. For their part the yeomanry claimed that they were attacked by the crowd, who were carrying 'revolutionary' banners. Certainly, having arrested Hunt, a cry went up from the yeomanry – 'Have at their flags!' – and they rode again into the crowd, this time in all directions, trying to seize the banners held aloft by some. They were soon enveloped in the fleeing crowd. Poor horsemanship and panic overtook some and they lashed out with the sharp edges of their swords. The crowd panicked also. Finally the magistrates, believing that the yeomanry were being attacked, ordered the 15th Hussars, a regular cavalry unit, to move to clear the crowds and rescue the yeomanry. The result was further panic and injury, although more by crushing than by the sabre, as the regulars followed their orders to use only 'flat of sword'. They swept all before them – crowd, constables and yeomanry:

> [The 15th Hussars] then pressed forward towards the Manchester Yeomanry. The people were in a state of utter rout and confusion, leaving the ground strewn with hats and shoes, and hundreds were thrown down in the attempt to escape. The cavalry were hurrying about in all directions, completing the work of dispersion . . . During the whole of this confusion shrieks . . . were heard in all directions, and as the crowd of people dispersed the effects of the conflict became visible. Some were seen bleeding on the ground and unable to rise; others, less seriously injured but faint with the loss of blood, were retiring slowly or leaning upon others for support . . . The whole of this extraordinary scene was the work of a few minutes.[10]

Eleven people were killed in the chaos and about four hundred injured, most by being crushed. The whole incident caused a great outcry and was dubbed 'Peterloo' in mocking tribute to the 'victory' of the military only four years after Waterloo. The use of yeomanry, undoubtedly less skilful and more class conscious and brutal in the work than regular cavalry, was a particular cause for criticism. In 1822 a test case was brought by one of the injured, Thomas Redford, against four members of the Manchester and Salford Yeomanry. A justification was pleaded to the effect that the assault was properly committed by the defendants in dispersing an unlawful assembly: this argument was accepted by the jury and the yeomen were found not guilty.[11] The government paid their expenses. However, the Manchester and Salford Yeomanry disbanded in 1824 amid much acrimony, and finally, in 1827, the government ordered a re-organisation which enforced what the 1816 regulations had encouraged – the amalgamation of individual troops of yeomanry into regiments of three or more troops, each troop to consist of not less than fifty men. This was a clear attempt to improve the training and

Portrait of Major Thomas Richmond Gale Braddyll, magistrate and owner of Conishead Priory near Ulverston, wearing the uniform of major, commanding the Lancashire corps of Yeomanry Cavalry, circa 1830. Braddyll was the driving force behind the uniting of the three remaining Lancashire yeomanry units in 1827, which timely decision probably ensured the survival of yeomanry in the county. A former Coldstream Guards officer, he had commanded the Furness Yeomanry (as a captain) since 1819. In 1834 he was made colonel, when the regiment was re-titled the Duke of Lancaster's Own Yeomanry.

responsibility of the yeomanry.

Amalgamation of Units

*I*n Lancashire the Bolton Yeomanry, the Furness Yeomanry and the Wigan Volunteer Light Horse (the only mounted volunteer units remaining in Lancashire in 1827) determined to unite under one command as the Bolton, Furness and Wigan Troops of a 'Lancashire Corps of Yeomanry Cavalry'. This was approved in 1828 and it is from this date that the modern Regiment can directly claim a descent, although, of course, through the Bolton element, it can be traced back further, to 1798.

Royal Honour

*F*inally, in 1834, William IV, who also held the title of Duke of Lancaster, authorised as a 'special act of favour' that the Regiment in future be known as the 'Duke of Lancaster's Own Corps of Yeomanry Cavalry'. From that day to this the Regiment toasts not 'the Queen' (or King) but 'the Duke of Lancaster'.[12]

The Regiment, three troops strong and numbering approximately 170, now began to make a notable impact (at least sufficient to gain coverage in the increasingly numerous local newspapers of Lancashire) whenever it assembled for regimental exercises and especially for the annual camp. Lancaster appears to have become the usual location for the camp in the 1830s, although in 1837, the year of Queen Victoria's accession, it is recorded that the three troops assembled at Blackpool, then a little-known backwater on the Fylde coast, whose sandy shore provided an ideal parade ground.

Chapter Two

Decade of Protest
1839–1848

'Plug' Riots

*I*n 1839 and throughout the 1840s civil unrest periodically returned. In some areas economic distress led to support for the Chartist movement, but in Lancashire the major causes of discontent were simply the attempts by factory- and mine-owners to reduce wages in the face of trade depression. In August 1842 several strikes occurred, becoming known as the 'plug' riots as the strikers (or 'turnouts') removed the plugs from mill boilers to prevent either fellow workers or blacklegs continuing to labour. Incidents occurred in Accrington, Ashton-under-Lyne, Blackburn, Bolton, Manchester, Oldham and Preston. Individual troops were called out 'in aid of the civil power' for these and other disturbances in this decade of protests, and two new troops were raised, at Rochdale in 1844 and Worsley in 1845. With either no, or only very small, organised police forces the authorities had little alternative but to call on locally-stationed regular army units (both cavalry and infantry), the yeomanry, and also temporarily to enrol numerous 'special constables'.

Call Out
1839 May – Furness and Wigan Troops at Bolton
1839 – Bolton Troop at Bolton
1840 – Wigan Troop at Wigan
1842 August – Wigan Troop at Preston and Blackburn
1842 August/September – Bolton Troop at Bolton
1842 August – Furness Troop at Blackburn and Accrington
1848 June – Bolton Troop at Bolton

'In Readiness'
1843 October
1848 July

THE RIOTS IN THE COUNTRY.

THE SCENE AT NEW CROSS.

Engraving from the *Illustrated London News* 1842 – 'The Riots in the Country'. This is New Cross, Manchester, but the scenes throughout Lancashire that year were, judging by newspaper accounts, similar – 'milling groups, some armed with tipstaves, make much noise but with no cohesion, and only isolated incidents result'.

Streets of Bolton

*T*he role of the local troop of yeomanry in Bolton in 1842 is particularly well recorded, and is worth chronicling at length as typical of the disturbances of the time. These were characterised by extensive rumours, threats and demands, intimidation and bluff, but surprisingly little physical injury or material damage. It was to combat just such threats – real and imagined – that the yeomanry owed its continued existence into the Victorian period. The two local Bolton newspapers, the *Chronicle* and the *Free Press*, offer sufficiently differing interpretations of events for us to feel that we can get close to the truth. The *Chronicle* was the staunch Tory paper, the *Free Press* more in sympathy with the demands, if not the methods, of the strikers.

Trouble first flared in early August in Manchester, Ashton, Oldham and Stalybridge. The first incident in Bolton occurred on Wednesday

10 August, when a meeting of the 'unemployed and distressed' was held in the evening at the market place.[13] Several hundred people attended. It was agreed that the next morning they would act in support of the events in Manchester and Ashton, and attempt to stop the mills and workshops. Their actions next day met with only mixed success, but a much larger crowd gathered, again in the market place, and appointed people to go to Blackburn, Chorley and Preston 'to urge the inhabitants to join their brethren in the great and glorious struggle'. Mills that refused to stop work when the 'turnouts' arrived were stoned. That night most of the mills were 'watched all night by the most trustworthy of the hands', and the magistrates swore in a number of special constables.

Friday 12 August saw increasing violence, with police assisting hands in defending mills under attack, and four people were arrested. The principal employers met at the Borough Court and resolved to keep their works open and to encourage their workpeople to be sworn in as special constables. A crowd carrying sticks and bludgeons, and led by colliers from the country, marched on the police office threatening to rescue the prisoners, but they were dispersed by the police.[14] The Mayor read the Riot Act and ordered inhabitants to keep indoors. The magistrates called for troops (25 men of the 72nd Highlanders with fixed bayonets) to assist in guarding the police office. At eight o'clock that evening news arrived of disturbances at Damside and Little Lever. The Bolton troop of yeomanry cavalry under Lieutenant John Fletcher was now called out and a detachment sent to Little Lever, the remainder joining the troops in guarding the police office throughout the night.[15]

On Saturday 13 August there was a further escalation of the disorder. At noon 'a mob consisting of about 5,000 persons, armed with bludgeons, staves, bars of iron, or anything else calculated to knock a man's brains out, enter[ed] the town, flourishing their weapons and giving loud hussas'. They had come principally from Bury, Heywood, Tottington and the surrounding neighbourhood.

> The mob presented a most formidable appearance and the weapons they carried were of a most deadly description. The language they used was exceedingly violent, levelled principally against the police, which body of men they swore they would murder before they left the town.

All the mills and workshops were stopped and shops closed. The Riot Act was read again but no serious confrontation occurred at the police office. Many of the mob, after stopping at the mills, had simply begged or demanded liquor, food and money, which they got, and then left. The town's gas lights were on all that night as a precaution.

Sunday was quiet. The police were employed in the evening delivering summonses to the registered electors, requiring them to attend next morning to be sworn in as special constables. The *Free Press* commented that:

> there was a very great reluctance evinced by the majority of the electors to take any part in the matter, the more ardent declared that they would not risk their lives, and incur popular odium, perhaps for life, to support a government and continue a state of things which had brought the people of these districts to this impoverished, alarming and desperate condition.

Monday 15 August saw a meeting of operative cotton spinners, who passed a revealing six-point resolution. They asked for the introduction of the political 'People's Charter', but this was only their fourth resolution. Primarily the cotton spinners attacked the wage reductions, poor housing, high rents and the employing of apprentices to do journeymen's work. They blamed the 'improvements of machinery, which have superseded manual labour, and created a redundant and burthensom population'. They saw salvation lying in two unrelated measures – the introduction of a Ten Hours Act to limit the hours of mill operation and, through emigration, wanted a policy 'to immediately colonize the Crown Lands, which would thus employ the redundant population, and at the same time improve and augment the home trade.

After resolving 'that delegates be appointed to meet those from others trades', they dispersed without incident, but another meeting held soon after led to a large group (two or three thousand strong) marching from Bolton towards Wigan to stop work there. Soon after, another group was reported marching towards Bolton. The *Free Press* takes up the story:

> The magistrates had previously held a meeting at the Swan Hotel, at which it had been resolved to oppose the entrance of this body into the town. Accordingly, when they had entered Bradshawgate, the military were ordered out, and in a few moments the cavalry, and a portion of the 72nd Highlanders, appeared in front of the Red Cross, headed by [four county magistrates and the Mayor] . . .
>
> The infantry were ordered to place themselves, two deep, across the street, with the cavalry close upon them. The crowd pressed on, cheering, the infantry were ordered to unfix bayonets and load, then came a trying and fearful moment, the soldiers were ordered to make ready and to present – the crowd then fell back, numbers deserting the main body, escaping by the back streets, throwing away their bludgeons and sticks. A body of police was then ordered to the front,

and the whole of the military, with the magistrates, advanced. The crowd fell back as the opposing party advanced, the former becoming weaker every moment, until they were effectually routed and dispersed . . .

The yeomanry galloped after the runaways, and many of them, in their haste, overthrew each other, and drove each other into the canal, where some of them remained some time up to the middle in water. One man was pushed into a reservoir belonging to the Springfield paper works, and there being some feet of mud there, he stuck fast and could not extricate himself without assistance.

The town continued in a very excited state for a considerable time after the dispersion of the party, and two or three times the yeomanry were engaged in clearing Bradshawgate. While doing this a person who seemed reluctant to move off at command was struck by J. Fletcher, Esq., lieutenant in the yeomanry, and wounded by a cut on the nose. The prisoners, having been committed for trial, were removed to the railway station under a strong escort of yeomanry, infantry, and police, and, we understand, that on their admission to the New Bailey, they were received by a cordial cheer from the inmates. At dusk a body of special constables marched from the police office and with the police, twice passed through the principal streets. At eleven o'clock all was peaceable.

The next day (Tuesday) things were quieter, despite its being the anniversary of Peterloo, a date previously marked by trouble. The yeomanry, police and infantry left the town and went to Halliwell following reports of disturbances, but did not find any serious rioting; nor did a detachment of yeomanry sent to Horwich. Wednesday morning, however, saw a crowd 'composed chiefly of women' stop a works in Bolton, withdrawing only when police and military arrived. Further excitement followed:

The next information of importance was the arrival of an express to the magistrates, announcing that a numerous body of men and boys from Heywood, Bury, and their neighbourhoods, were making an attack on the collieries of J. Fletcher, Esq., at Lady Shore, the works at Little Lever, and Mount Zion, near Radcliffe. About half the troop of yeomanry were sent off, and in an hour or two after an express arrived, desiring that a strong escort might be sent down to Little Lever, to bring up a large number of prisoners, who had been taken. The remainder of the yeomanry, the police, and all the infantry, excepting a guard of about twelve men, were sent off immediately in that direction . . . Soon after seven o'clock, Bradshawgate was a scene of great excitement, in consequence of the arrival of the military and police with seven carts and a wagon filled with prisoners

16

from Little Lever etc. [There were 79 prisoners in all.] A few stones were thrown at them as they passed up the street. Some thousands of spectators were assembled in that street, the neighbouring streets, and about the police office. The prisoners were all labouring men and youths, from fifteen to fifty years of age, and most of them had a neglected and distressed appearance. After they had been searched, and the usual particulars respecting them been taken down, they were all arraigned before the county magistrates, and evidence given that Mr. Fletcher's works had been attacked, stopped, and injury done to them. The prisoners formed part of the crowd, and had been followed and watched until the military came up, surrounded, and took them prisoners . . .

The prisoners being asked if they wished to make any statement, about a dozen of them stepped out, and all gave the same account, that they had no intention of doing any harm, but had left home through curiosity, and then been forced by the 'crew'. With one exception, all that spoke said they came from Heywood . . . A young man, named James McNichol, was then placed at the bar, and Cuthbert Baines, one of the yeomanry, stated that when coming up Bradshawgate with the prisoners, the prisoner called out 'cabbage cutters!'.[16] He (witness) told him to hold his noise and go home. The prisoner then pulled from his pocket a bullet or ball, and said he'd stick that into him before that night passed. He gave information to Holden, one of the police, who took him into custody. Holden stated that the prisoner was once rescued from him, and was not taken without great difficulty. [He had] found no ball or ammunition upon him. Prisoner said he came from Egerton, and was a shoemaker. He denied that he had shown any ball . . .

[They were] told that they all stood committed for trial . . . They were then removed and placed in carts, escorted as before to the railway station, where a special train waited to convey them to the New Bailey. The special constables, having assembled, accompanied the military, and afterwards paraded the streets. At ten o'clock quietness was once more restored in the town.

After such activity Thursday proved to be another day of wild rumour but little event, and Friday was even quieter. In fact, the drama was now almost played out. On the following Tuesday (23 August) a last alarm was sounded which proved to be, in the words of the *Chronicle*, an 'unintentional hoax':

On Tuesday last, it was arranged that signals should be given from the neighbouring mills by telegraphic despatches, in case of the approach of the mob, and that they should be answered from the steeple of the parish church. A flag for the purpose was placed in readiness at the works of Messrs. Heyes, Hamer and Jackson, Burnden, and about five o'clock, some of the workmen thought they would try how it would act, and for that purpose wound it up the pole. The man upon the parish church observing it thought it was a signal denoting the approach of a body of rioters and immediately hoisted an answer that troops would be forthcoming. A bell was tolled, warning the special and other constables, and the military and a large body of police were immediately under arms and on their way towards Farnworth, and on their arrival there, could not find either a disturbance or the intelligence of one having been committed, and returned to the town about an hour afterwards, mortified at the hoax, but pleased that they had not the unpleasant task of suppressing a riot.

The *Free Press* had a more entertaining account:

In the evening some alarm was occasioned by the hoisting of a flag on the steeple of the Parish Church, then calling out of the military and police, and their marching off at a rapid rate towards the Manchester road, accompanied by W.F. Hulton, Esq. To the inquiry 'What's to do now?' the answer was, some disturbance has arisen towards Halshaw Moor and at Messrs. Crompton's works. It proved happily to be a false alarm, originating through some blunder or mistake of the man on the steeple of Farnworth church, who inadvertently raised his signal and caused the commotion. Some jokes were passed on the affair; one wag said the man had seen an Oddfellow's funeral within view, and had mistaken the carriers of the mutes and funeral staves for the sticks and bludgeons of the rioters.

This paper records for the same day a suspected act of arson at a barn, one of the last acts of the disturbances. Gradually the strikers drifted back to work, and the unemployed and distressed into acquiescence with their lot (or perhaps into realisation of their inability to force change). There were rumours that wages would actually increase but, as the *Free Press* records, this was far from settled:

On Thursday morning the remainder of the cotton spinning and power-loom mills were opened, and the hands went to work, the masters refusing to make any advance on their wages, saying they must first return to work, and if they thought proper to strike against their present wages, to give proper notice of it, and then they would consider it. The police are now restored to their accustomed beats during the night, and some are on their usual duty in the day. The town has quite resumed its ordinary appearance. The cavalry are still in quarters, but we hope soon to hear of their dismissal to their homes.

In fact the Bolton troop of yeomanry cavalry were not stood down until 8 September.

A Bad Popular Image

T *he* yeomanry were undoubtedly better trained and more able to deal with the 'Plug' and 'Chartist' riots than they had been twenty years before, at 'Peterloo'. There was no loss of life involving the DLOY at Bolton in 1842. They remained, however, the subject of much popular derision and suspicion. The *Bolton Free Press,* for example, could not let this incident during the 1842 riots pass without comment:

When the civil and military forces were clearing Bradshawgate on Monday, one of the 'bold yeomen' left the ranks to pursue an old woman who could not escape either easily or speedily. In her haste and agitation her cap fell from her head, and her grey hairs streamed in the wind. The sight had such a ludicrous cast, that a universal laugh of derision resounded from every side, even from the yeomanry themselves, and the zealous trooper returned to his place.

The same paper had shown a similar attitude towards the unit earlier in 1842 when the yeomanry went on their annual training: 'The Bolton troop of this body of 'irregular horse' left this town on Thursday morning, for eight days' exercise at Lancaster. It is expected that on their return, they will volunteer for service in India; so, 'Look out, Afghans!'.

In 1844 the *Free Press* was still uncomplimentary:

The Bolton Troop of the above corps (corpses some readers will pronounce it, and very like resuscitated corpses some of the corps looked) left this town on Thursday morning, for a week's training and exercise at Lancaster, where, we suppose, they will be joined by the Wigan and Furness troops. The military and pensioners should be on the alert, now that from this town is withdrawn the protecting power of so many brawny hands and heroic hearts.

Upon their return:

The 'Lumber Troop' returned from their week's spree at Lancaster . . . from the fact that there was a led horse without a rider in the ranks it was feared by some old women that one of the heroes had fallen a victim to his ardour for military distinction and national

19

glory, but, on enquiry [it was] found that the whole troop had passed through the critical campaign without the loss of a single man or a married man either.

The raising of a new troop for the DLOY at Rochdale in the same year led to similar hostile comment from a monthly periodical entitled *The Spectator: a Rochdale Miscellany*, which saw their raising as a political act. Note the reference to Peterloo, still fresh in the mind after 25 years:

> The formation of such a Corps in Rochdale is a foul and colmnunious [sic] imputation on the loyalty of its inhabitants, and an outrageous insult to their good sense and love of order. The plea of necessity is not valid in a period of peace; the Public Good is not to be ensured by standing armies of soldiery; and private interests are equally incompatible with the devotion of their time to the follies of a mock-soldier's life . . . If these swords are ever to be fleshed, a shudder creeps over the poor artisan, that he perhaps, may be one of the victims! It is too well remembered by the Inhabitants of this Parish, although a quarter of a century has elapsed, what cruelties and excesses an infuriated Corps of Tory Yeomanry committed in a

"KEEPING A GOOD FACE TOWARDS THE ENEMY,"

Woodcut cartoon: 'Keeping a Good Face Towards the Enemy'.

neighbouring town; and the Rochdale Volunteers, with one exception, are all of the same political party, and own as few redeeming qualities for kindness and good-feeling as their predecessors.

The raising of a further DLOY troop at Worsley in the following year (1845) seemed to cause less local comment. Worsley also became the site of the first formal Regimental Headquarters for the still-growing regiment.

Raising of the Lancashire Hussars

*I*n 1848, the year of revolutions across mainland Europe, an entire second regiment of yeomanry cavalry was formed in Lancashire. Entitled the 'Lancashire Hussar Regiment of Yeomanry Cavalry', it was raised by Sir John Gerard of Garswood New Hall, near Wigan. The first troop, of 75 men, was raised principally from Sir John's tenantry in the neighbourhood of Garswood and Ashton-in-Makerfield, with others from Aspull, Billinge and Wigan. A second troop of similar size was raised shortly afterwards, with men from St.

Southport 1899 – DLOY parade. Note the Hussar officer.

Helens, Windle, Ormskirk and Liverpool. Further growth followed later. Sir John became the first Commanding Officer, continuing a family tradition, since the Gerards had previously raised the Ashton Volunteer Cavalry, which served from 1798 to 1823. Sir John provided at his own expense superior swords and uniform fittings, and from the start they were a superbly turned-out regiment.[17]

On Sir John Gerard's death in 1854 his brother Robert succeeded to both the estate and, such was the nature of the yeomanry regiments even at this late date, to the command of the Lancashire Hussars.

In 1855 the Hussars trained together with the 'Duke's Own' in Liverpool – a rare occasion when the DLOY forsook Lancaster. In 1856 they again trained together, this time at Lancaster. In 1857 they went their separate ways for annual camps but were to retain a close connection (not to say rivalry), occasionally conducting joint training, and when the Hussars were converted to artillery in 1921 those members who wished to remain in a mounted regiment were allowed to transfer to the 'Duke's Own' without loss of seniority.

Chapter Three

Pomp and Circumstance 1849–1899

Royal Duties

*T*he next fifty years of the Regiment's history were quiet; a direct result of rapid formation of borough and then county police forces. There was no call for active service from the Regiment over the whole of this period, as far as is known, although the Lancashire Hussars were briefly called out during local disturbances in 1853 at Aspull and Haigh, near Wigan, and in 1868 at Skelmersdale.[18] Duties were largely ceremonial, detachments in review order providing escorts and guards of honour at royal events, both national and local.

Local

1851	October	Visit by Queen Victoria and the Prince Consort to Worsley.
1857	June	Visit by Queen Victoria and the Prince Consort to Manchester.[19]
1869	July	Visit by the Prince of Wales to Worsley.
1894	May	Visit by Queen Victoria for the opening of the Manchester Ship Canal.
1897	July	Visit by the Duke of York (future King George) to Manchester.

National

1897	June	Queen Victoria's Diamond Jubilee Procession in London.

The Regiment also regularly provided a Guard for the High Sheriff of Lancashire, while the highlight of the year was undoubtedly the annual camp, when the training in horsemanship and musketry could be shown off in competition between individuals and between the troops of the Regiment.

ARRIVAL OF H.R.H. PRINCE ALBERT AT THE ART-TREASURES PALACE, MANCHESTER.

Engraving from the *Illustrated London News*, 1857, showing the arrival of HRH Prince Albert at the Art-Treasures Palace in Manchester, accompanied by the DLOY mounted escort.

Yeomanry Criticised

Not surprisingly, many saw the yeomanry increasingly as an expensive luxury. In 1857 payment by the government for training days was stopped. However, many commanders took to paying the yeomanry themselves, while the yeomanry had a powerful friend in the Duke of Cambridge, who was Commander-in-Chief of the army from 1856 to 1895. The Crimean War (1853–1856) saw the yeomanry fill a recognised role as a home defence force, in a conflict that so stretched the resources of the regular forces that some militia battalions (an auxiliary force that at this date was actually composed only of volunteers) were sent to replace garrison troops in the Mediterranean. Meanwhile French intentions were causing increasing unease with an ambitious naval building programme endorsed by Emperor Napoleon III, nephew of Napoleon I. In 1859 a great expansion of the British volunteer forces occurred, from which the yeomanry benefited greatly. Most of the growth was in infantry volunteer rifle corps, which proved a great success and brought a new

The earliest known photograph of the Officers of the Regiment (1862). The photograph was taken in three sections.

respectability to voluntary military service in general. In Lancashire two units of 'Light Horse Volunteers' were also raised, in 1860 and 1862, but did not prove long-lasting, probably because they duplicated the role of the two existing yeomanry regiments.

Gradually the government imposed a greater regulation on the yeomanry. In 1870 new rulings were issued, further defining the size of yeomanry regiments and the nature of their training, and fixing the establishment at 36 regiments throughout the country. The next year overall responsibility for the yeomanry was taken from the County Lieutenants and given to the Secretary of State for War, and the granting of officers' commissions came under the Crown, as in the Regular Army. In 1888 the yeomanry without exception became liable for service anywhere in Britain in the event of invasion, and in 1893 all yeomanry cavalry regiments were ordered to re-organise on a squadron basis.

Much remained archaic, however. Breech-loading carbines became standard issue in 1870 but the inspecting officer's reports for the latter years of the century continued to show an excessive interest in the requirements for sword exercises and set-piece manoeuvres. The lessons offered by conflicts such as the American Civil War and the Franco-Prussian War did lead to change, but it was always a slow progress.

Continued Growth

*T*he yeomanry may have led a quiet life compared to the earlier part of the century, but the 'Duke's Own' did not lack for volunteers. The five troops of the Regiment in 1849 – Bolton, Furness, Rochdale, Wigan and Worsley – were joined by Oldham in 1872, Broughton (Manchester) in 1877, Blackburn in 1880, and Blackpool and Liverpool in 1899.[20] The only disbandments were of the Furness Troop in 1872 and the Wigan Troop in 1883, so that by the end of the century the Regiment was at probably its greatest strength to date. Organised as eight troops in four squadrons, with Regimental Headquarters still at Worsley, it was around five hundred strong.

The squadrons comprised:

'A' Squadron:	Oldham and Rochdale Troops
'B' Squadron:	Liverpool and Bolton Troops
'C' Squadron:	Broughton and Worsley Troops
'D' Squadron:	Blackburn and Blackpool Troops

Annual Camps

*F*or most of the Victorian period the annual camp continued to be held at Lancaster.[21] The 'Duke's Own' were welcomed by the townspeople, especially by the tradesmen, who favourably noted that the continuing requirement for members to provide their own horses meant that even the 'other ranks' of the 'Duke's Own' were usually of some private means, especially when compared with the rankers in the Royal Lancashire Militia, who on occasion also camped at Lancaster. In fact, little had changed since Napoleonic times, with the majority of recruits still from farming or the more prosperous urban trades, with the larger landowners or their urban counterparts serving as officers.

In 1893 the Regiment moved camp to Southport, where an excellent drill ground was found in the wide expanse of the sands, which had been used for many years by the Lancashire Hussars. Camps were repeated here each year for the rest of the century, excepting 1896, when Carlisle was the venue for a combined training with the Westmorland and Cumberland Yeomanry.

Southport, 1899. The Regiment parades with its drums on the firm sands near Birkdale, as spectators watch.

Old Soldiers

M *ounted* drill standards at the annual camp were high – only keen horsemen were wanted in the 'Duke's Own' and in these aspects of training they were, in the nineteenth century, little if anything behind the regulars. Indeed some of their members had seen service in the regular army. It was not uncommon for cavalry officers who retired early to obtain commissions in the yeomanry and each regiment, at least by the 1850s, had its cadre of instructors who were NCOs of the regular army serving on attachment, or recently retired. Two of the best known of these in the DLOY were Regimental Sergeant-Major Adams and Sergeant-Major Williams; the former a veteran of Waterloo and the latter a survivor of the Charge of the Light Brigade.

John Adams was probably the longest serving member in the history of the 'Duke's Own'. After serving for 22 years in the 1st

Sgt. Major Adams in uniform, wearing his Waterloo Medal, circa 1860. In 1863 he gained a second award – the Long Service and Good Conduct Medal.

Sgt. Major Richard Hall Williams, a survivor of the Charge of the Light Brigade.

(King's) Dragoon Guards he retired in 1827 as troop sergeant-major with a pension. In 1828, however, he entered the Bolton Troop of the DLOY (then known as the Lancashire Yeomanry Cavalry) as sergeant instructor, becoming troop sergeant-major in 1830. In 1849 he transferred to the Worsley troop (formed only in 1845) and was subsequently made regimental sergeant-major, being the first to hold that rank in the regiment. He was still serving at the time of his death in 1876, aged 92. Such figures were beloved by the Victorian public, who held them up as shining examples to their youth. As the newspaper report of his funeral stated, 'Altogether the gallant veteran had served his country for the prolonged period of nearly 72 years'.[22] He was apparently wounded at the Battle of Waterloo, where his horse was killed, but 'he instantly seized another horse which had lost its old rider, a French cuirassier, and upon this he rode in the subsequent stages of the strife'. He proudly wore his medal for service at Waterloo on his yeomanry uniform together with, after 1863, a long service and good conduct medal.

In command of the firing party at Adams' impressive military funeral in 1876 was Sergeant-Major Williams, who had himself led an eventful previous career in the regular cavalry. Richard Hall Williams served with the 17th Lancers during the campaigns of the Crimea and the Indian Mutiny. He took part in the Battles of Inkerman, Alma and Sebastopol and rode in the Charge of the Light Brigade at Balaclava on 25 October 1854. He was discharged from regular service in 1867, aged 58, and at the recommendation of the Earl of Ellesmere joined the Worsley Troop as Drill Sergeant. Williams was postmaster of Worsley, and drill took place in the meadow behind his house. He was a colourful character, with a passion for drill movements to music – on horseback, dismounted and with the sabre. These extended beyond the troop to the children of Worsley, including those of the Commanding Officer, the Earl of Ellesmere; girls on one day, and boys on another. His most famous tale concerned his survival during the Charge of the Light Brigade. Apparently he had a severe abscess on his nose and, prior to the action, tied a blood-stained bandage around his face:

> My visage was so fearsome that the Russians held their fire . . . But pain was such that the following day I must report to the Regimental Surgeon: a step not taken lightly in the Regiment: two orderlies hold me and I receive a smart buffet on the nose which disperses the fluid.

In 1877 the Worsley Troop presented him with an inscribed sword in recognition of his long service: which was not, apparently, about to end! The date of his final retirement is unknown, and it is quite possible that he retained some training role within the Regiment into advanced old age. Certainly when he died in 1910 (aged 91) large crowds from Worsley, including the yeomanry, turned out to follow his coffin.[23]

There was no official ruling given as to the age limits for yeomanry service before 1889, when it was stated that officers should normally retire at sixty, although this could be extended, on recommendation, to 67; other ranks were to be not less than seventeen and not above 49 years of age. The retirement of active, permanent-staff NCOs remained, however, a 'grey area' into this century. To the Victorian military mind such characters merely improved with age!

Volunteers for War

*T*he long period without active service came to an end for many yeomanry volunteers with the outbreak of the Second Boer War in southern Africa in 1899 and the formation of a new mounted infantry force known as 'The Imperial Yeomanry'. One hundred and twenty-two men formerly in the 'Duke's Own' successfully volunteered to serve overseas; 102 were to serve with the 23rd Company, 8th Battalion, Imperial Yeomanry – enough to enable the unit to adopt the subtitle 'Duke of Lancaster's Own' and to earn for the parent regiment the battle honour 'South Africa 1900–1902'.

Chapter Four

The 23rd (Duke of Lancaster's Own) Company, Imperial Yeomanry, in Southern Africa 1900–1902

British confident at start

*T*he origins of the Boer War (technically the Second Boer War) were complex. Suffice it to say here that the British expected the war with the two Boer Republics of the Transvaal and the Orange Free State to be quickly over. After all, the Boers (descendants of the early Dutch settlers) numbered at most sixty thousand fighting men, while Britain had all the resources of an Empire embracing one quarter of the world's population. An army corps of fifty thousand men was sent to southern Africa, with little expectation of a long conflict.

The British military planners were soon forced to think again. In both tactics and composition the army corps was shown to be unsuited and suffered several early defeats. The Boer proved to be a new and dangerous kind of opponent for a British army whose recent experience (and training) had been restricted to overcoming poorly-armed opposition in small colonial wars. The Boer was a crack shot, and preferred to fight with skirmishes rather than large battles. After an action the expert Boer horseman would ride quickly away across sandy, infertile and almost waterless desert, where no infantry could follow. The British needed to use similar tactics of mounted reconnaissance and dismounted skirmishing to defeat such a swift and mobile enemy. But only ten per cent of the early British force was mounted, and they were regular cavalry who expected to fight on horseback with sabre and lance rather than on foot with rifle, so there was an urgent need for mounted men who could also shoot well. The existing yeomanry in Britain were one obvious source.

Formation of the Imperial Yeomanry

O n 20 December 1899, a War Office Order stated that 'Her Majesty's Government have decided to raise for service in South Africa a mounted infantry force to be named "The Imperial Yeomanry" '. It was hoped to recruit many men from the ranks of the existing yeomanry, but provision was also made for others with riding and shooting ability to be enlisted as well.

Uniform was to be 'Norfolk jackets of woollen materials of neutral colour, breeches and gaiters, lace boots and felt hats. Strict uniformity of pattern will not be insisted on'.

Many men in the existing yeomanry regiments did volunteer. Thus was formed the 23rd Company, Imperial Yeomanry, sub-titled the 'Duke of Lancaster's Own', as volunteers from the 'Duke's Own' and others were formally enlisted at the Town Hall in Chorlton. Having been sworn in and medically examined, they moved to Blackpool early in January 1900, for training and kitting out prior to sailing for the Cape.

The 23rd (Duke of Lancaster's Own) Company, Imperial Yeomanry, had only four weeks in which to train at Blackpool. The horses owned and previously ridden by the men were considered in

The 23rd (DLOY) Company, Imperial Yeomanry, drill on Blackpool Beach. The event was watched by crowds from the promenade. (Central Pier is just visible in the background.)

'B' Troop, 23rd (DLOY) Company, Imperial Yeomanry, outside Blackpool Town Hall, 1900. Note how the Town Hall was still under construction at this time.

the main unsuitable for campaigning, and new horses were provided by the War Office, or donated by generous individuals. Much hard training, despite snow, rain and fog, was necessary to familiarise horse and rider.

Lee-Enfield rifles were issued, an infantry weapon carried to stress their 'mounted infantry' role, and learning to handle these long and cumbersome arms also took time. Each troop made use of the rifle ranges at Fleetwood, travelling by tramcar most of the way and marching the rest. Some of the men failed shooting tests and were replaced by other volunteers from a large reserve list. Two rapid-firing Colt guns were also added to the equipment, served by a specially formed gun-section of sixteen men and one officer.

The men readily found board and lodging in the out-of-season resort, and the town generously gave them free admission to many amusements – music hall shows at the Alhambra and pantomimes at the Grand Theatre and Opera House were especially popular. A farewell dinner was organised at the Alhambra by the town mayor, while the Grand Theatre held a 'Grand Fashionable and Patriotic Night' to mark their departure.

A large crowd gathered to see the volunteers aboard ship at Liverpool's Canada Dock, although it was a wintry day with snow on the ground. Special trains were provided for family and friends to attend, and bands played as the men and horses embarked; *Soldiers of the Queen*, *The girl I left behind me*, and *Auld Lang Syne* ensured an emotional send-off.[24]

The White Star cargo-passenger ship *Afric* was only recently built. She sailed at 8.30 that evening, Sunday 11 February 1900. The 24th (Westmorland and Cumberland Yeomanry) Company shared the accommodation, and would serve with the 23rd in southern Africa, both being part of the 8th Battalion of the Imperial Yeomanry.

Conditions on board were good, since this was a regular scheduled passage and not specially hired as a troopship. The men slept four to a cabin in the style of second-class passengers, while the horses were placed in temporary wooden stalls.[25]

The voyage of over six thousand miles took exactly three weeks, the *Afric* arriving outside Table Bay, Cape Town on Sunday 3 March 1900. For the first time in history, men of the 'Duke's Own' were overseas – and at war.

After two months in camp for men and horses to get used to the new climate, the 23rd Company, together with the 24th, went by train to the

SOUTHERN AFRICA 1900-1902

interior. At Belmont, near the Orange Free State border, they joined a force under General Sir Charles Warren, for the suppression of those Boers who had occupied towns in the district of Griqualand West, for this was the time of British counter-offensives.

Camp at Faber's Put

*W*ithin days they experienced what was to be their fiercest battle of the war. On the night of 29 May 1900 they camped near a farm called Faber's Put. The camp was positioned between two large, square cattle enclosures with low stone walls, known as *kraals*, into which the horses were put. The men camped in their troops, each troop forming a circle out of saddles, within which the men slept. Lookouts were posted.

Also part of the force was a detachment of four guns from the Canadian Artillery and three companies of the Duke of Edinburgh's Own Volunteer Rifles – a unit raised in Cape Colony. General Warren and his staff occupied the farmhouse. Finally, a twelve-man patrol of 'Paget's Horse', also part of the Imperial Yeomanry, joined the camp just before last light, and camped near to one of the *kraals*.

Just before dawn next morning, after reveille had sounded but while all was still quiet, the camp was suddenly saturated with a hail of small arms fire. Men threw off their blankets, grabbed bandoliers and sheltered behind their saddles. The camp was attacked from several angles, in a well planned attack; the Boers had approached with great care, and the sentries had seen nothing. The firing frightened the horses in the *kraals* and a stampede started.

The Boers were mainly concentrated in a group of small trees and bushes near one of the *kraals* and near to the Colt guns. As it grew lighter these guns were used with some effect, but already the Boers were retiring. Without horses on which to pursue them, it was left to the Canadian Artillery to fire the last few rounds of the battle.

It was a short and indecisive exchange. If the Boers expected, as prisoners claimed, that the volunteer and largely untried Imperial Yeomanry would flee under fire so that the Canadian guns could be captured, then they were very much mistaken. Equally, however, the camp arrangements were revealed to be dangerously inadequate. But for the Colt guns, whose presence evidently surprised the Boers, a dangerous situation might have arisen. As it was, casualties were 22 killed and 32 wounded, including six dead and eleven wounded for the 23rd Company. The Boers had similar casualties, mostly in the area of the trees and bushes, and caused by the Colt guns late in the action. Their raiding force included both boys and grey-haired farmers.

Action near Hoopstad and Luckoff

*F*aber's Put was the most serious action in which the 23rd Company were engaged during their time in southern Africa, but there were several lesser skirmishes, such as an action near Hoopstad when the rear of a British column they were protecting was ambushed. Two men of the 23rd Company were wounded.

In November 1900 the Yeomanry were sent to aid several beseiged town garrisons further to the west, well inside the Orange Free State. Near Luckoff (a place rapidly re-named by the British soldiers), a force of over seven hundred Boers was briefly engaged and then with some success pursued as the Boers tried to retire.

The strategy was continually to harry the Boers after any action, to force them from the areas they knew well. Boer farms were burned and Boer families were collected together in large camps, with the aim of totally isolating the Boer guerilla. It was a harsh policy, but in time proved effective. It became increasingly difficult for the Boers to recruit and assemble large forces for surprise actions.

Move to Cape Colony – and home

*J*ust before Christmas 1900 the Yeomanry were moved south, back into British Cape Colony. Here the patrolling and garrisoning continued. Occasional shots were exchanged with snipers and chases ensued, but mainly it was a case of simply being present in this British area to deter Boer raiding parties from the north.

About April 1901, orders were received to return to England, as a relief contingent had been raised at home, again with a large proportion of men from the 'Duke's Own'. A few chose to stay in Cape Colony – to start new lives, or to continue the adventure with the new draft, or in other units.

Relief Contingent

T *his* second group had a particularly wearisome time in Cape Colony – the routine work of constant patrolling mixed with the ever-present threat of ambush and snipers. A brief action at Middleport left four dead or dying, and six wounded, but the major actions of the later stages of the war occurred in other areas.

The war finally ended in May 1902, when the Treaty of Vereeniging absorbed the Transvaal and the Orange Free State into the British Empire, but with the promise of future Boer self-government. Thus ended the first overseas service of men of the 'Duke's Own'.

In recognition of the fact that 122 men from the Regiment had served overseas, 102 of them in the 23rd Company, 8th Imperial Yeomanry, the 'Duke's Own' were granted the battle honour 'South Africa 1900–1902'. This, the first battle honour, was added to the regimental drum banner and was a fitting tribute to the service of the Regiment's volunteers, five of whom had been killed and six wounded in action, with three others dead by disease or accident.

Chapter Five

Last Years of Peace 1900–1914

Some Lessons Learnt

T he new and temporary 'Imperial Yeomanry' proved to be of great value as mounted infantry in southern Africa, and this led to changes in the official attitude towards the established yeomanry in Britain even while the war was in progress. In 1901 new regulations gave each regiment a fixed official strength and added 'Imperial' to their titles. These changes can be summarised as follows:

1. All regiments to be of uniform strength – 596 of all ranks divided into four squadrons and a machine gun section.
2. A horse allowance of £5 per man to be paid.
3. The standard rifle to be the Lee Enfield magazine rifle with bayonet.
4. All sword exercises to be abolished.

Drill was simplified and training was to be as mounted infantry with the accent on scouting techniques. It was also stipulated that any regiment failing after a reasonable time to maintain 420 'efficient enrolled members', or any squadron with less than a hundred 'efficients', would be liable for disbandment. The 'Duke's Own', in fact, had no difficulty in recruiting, especially after the horse allowance which encouraged recruitment of non-horseowners, who could now hire their mounts when required. A waiting list was apparently the norm for most troops.

The new legislation, whilst maintaining the liability of yeomanry volunteers to be called out at times of invasion or other national emergency, also extended this liability to all British possessions in Europe. Training periods were to be not greater than seventeen days' duration, or less than fourteen days, in any one year.

Thus was created the 'Duke of Lancaster's Own Imperial Yeomanry', or 'DLOIY'. The War Office now involved itself closely with the Regiment, anxious that mounted infantry as well as cavalry

A DLOIY Trooper wearing khaki and mounted on a cob horse, circa 1903.

skills should be brought into training. Now that a horse allowance was given, recruits increasingly came from the industrial centres and were taught to ride from scratch, rather than farmers' or tradesmen's sons with their own or their employers' mounts. This trend also enabled the War Office to insist that the 'Duke's Own' be equipped with smaller and sturdier horses, 'cobs' that were less attractive than the previous 'chargers', but more suitable for long campaigning and rapid dismounting in action.

Problems Remain

U *ndoubtedly* the Regiment became better organised and altogether more serious of purpose in the aftermath of the Boer War experience of so many of its members, although the turnover of recruits was high and the experienced men did not, it seems, generally stay for long. Between 1904 and 1908 an 'Imperial Yeomanry Long Service and Good Conduct Medal' was awarded to those with over ten years' service and with an attendance at a minimum of ten annual

NCOs' pose outside their bell tent, after presentation of IY LSGC medals in Lowther Park, Cumberland, 1905.

camps – only twenty men in the DLOIY ever proved eligible. Moreover, the numerous volunteer military units, including the yeomanry, remained only loosely organised between themselves. Standards of equipment and training might be rising generally but were still varied, and the precise wartime role of the volunteers was still not clear. In 1908 further large scale reforms of the volunteers sought to mould all together into a more obvious and effective military force. A new army, the 'Territorial Force', was created to embrace all the volunteer units.

The Territorial Force

*W*ith a strength of 300,000 men this was designed to defend the United Kingdom if the regular forces were overseas, and was militarily self-sufficient. It included its own infantry, artillery and

41

Presentation of the first Guidon to the DLOY by King Edward VII, Worsley Park, 1909.

The DLOY sample the delights of unfamiliar modern transport, circa 1910. The vehicle registration indicates the Manchester area, so this is probably an excursion in a hired vehicle from the RHQ at Worsley.

mounted troops. Recruitment was locally based, with each region having its own division. The volunteers were committed to serve anywhere in the United Kingdom but service abroad at time of mobilisation was not compulsory. Attendance at an annual training camp for a fortnight was required, meanwhile, in peacetime. The yeomanry, who now dropped 'Imperial' from their titles, became the cavalry-cum-mounted infantry of this force, with the same conditions of service and training. The DLOY thus became divisional cavalry to the 42nd (East Lancashire) Division (Territorial Force).

At an impressive ceremony in 1909 Edward VII presented the Regiment with its first standard. The venue was Worsley Park on 6th July; a crowd of over a hundred thousand gathered to see a Royal Review of the 42nd Division, during which colours were presented to the new infantry battalions, and the light cavalry equivalent, the Guidon, to the DLOY.

Another change was the move of the Regimental Headquarters from Worsley, where it had been for over half a century; the new location from 1914 was on Whalley Road, Whalley Range, where a large residence was christened 'Lancaster House'.

Pomp and Ceremony

*D*etachments of the 'Duke's Own' continued to perform ceremonial duties such as royal escorts and guards of honour for events both local and national, the dashing uniforms making them ideal for such occasions.

1901	February	Funeral Procession of Queen Victoria in London.
1902	March	Visit by the Prince and Princess of Wales (later King George V and Queen Mary) to Manchester to open the Whitworth Hall and to unveil a statue of the late Queen Victoria at the Cathedral.
1902	August	Coronation Procession of King Edward VII in London.
1904	July	Visit by King Edward VII and Queen Alexandra to Liverpool to lay the foundation stone of the new Anglican Cathedral.
1905	July	Visit by King Edward VII to Salford.
1908	October	Unveiling of the Boer War Memorial, St Ann's Square, Manchester.
1910	May	Funeral Procession of King Edward VII in London.

Mounted Escort provided by the DLOIY at Salford, July 1905, for a visit by King Edward VII.

1911   June   Coronation Procession of King George V in London.[26]

1913   July   Visit by King George V and Queen Mary to Manchester.

The DLOY also regularly provided a Guard for the High Sheriff of Lancashire and there were many other appearances at local events. Probably the last ceremonial duty before the outbreak of the First World War took place in May 1914, when a detachment attended a Territorial Force church parade and march past in Liverpool.

Annual Training Camps

*T*he annual camp was always the highlight of the year for the 'Duke's Own' but never more so than in the years just before 1914, as they trained with other units of the 42nd Division – a vast gathering of men, all volunteers from the North West region.

View of the Squadron dining tent, during the camp at Lowther Park, May 1912.

Annual camp at Greystoke, Cumberland, June 1913. A Vickers-Maxim machine-gun is displayed alongside the tent and horse-lines.

In 1909 the DLOY had their first experience of Salisbury Plain, an event made the more memorable by thunderstorms that blew down tents and, more seriously, caused a stampede from the horse lines.

The DLOY now trained largely as mounted infantry, but also retained an expertise as mounted mobile scouts, able to observe and silently report, as occasion demanded. Both skills were to be much employed in the coming world war.

Weekly drill nights and regular weekend training days were, of course, also a feature of yeomanry life, then as now. Thus it was only on Monday 3 August 1914, a bank holiday and the day before war was declared, that the DLOY's last peacetime training took place. A tactical exercise was held near Knutsford, with the Cheshire Yeomanry acting as the enemy on bicycle and horseback.[27] There is no information as to the outcome of the exercise – probably few minded, as greater world events came to the fore.

Chapter Six

The First World War
1914–1918

Introduction

O *n* the evening of 4 August 1914, the day war was declared, the orders for mobilisation of the DLOY were sent out. The Regiment was already up to strength but further equipment had to be obtained and horses purchased. It soon became clear that this conflict was on an unprecedented scale and that the Territorial Force was needed abroad more than it was at home. The men of the 42nd Division were asked to volunteer for service overseas, and 90% readily did so.

It was the first time that the Regiment itself had gone abroad and to war, although the Regiment was actually to serve divided between Europe and the Middle East. Men of 'A' and 'B' Squadrons embarked for Egypt with the 42nd Division, but the Regimental Headquarters and 'C' and 'D' Squadrons went to France. The men of 'B' Squadron were not, in fact, to serve under that title in the 42nd Division – the Bolton Troop was absorbed into the Divisional Military Mounted Police, whilst the Liverpool Troop joined 'A' Squadron to bring it up to war establishment when it was ordered to Egypt.[28]

Egypt and Palestine

T *he* men of 'A' and 'B' Squadrons sailed for Egypt on the night of 10/11 September 1914. The 42nd (East Lancashire) Division was the first territorial division to leave England. It had been expected that the whole Regiment would accompany the Division but finally only the men of these two squadrons were ordered to embark.

In Egypt the Division was to protect the strategically vital Suez Canal. Although Britain was still at peace with Turkey it was feared

47

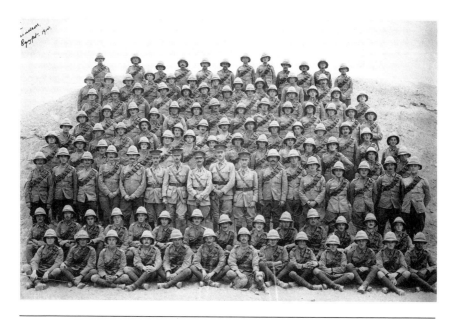

'A' Squadron in Egypt, 1914, probably soon after arrival.

Shaving in the desert near the Suez Canal, February 1915. This splendid 'candid' image was taken by one of the officers with an illicit camera.

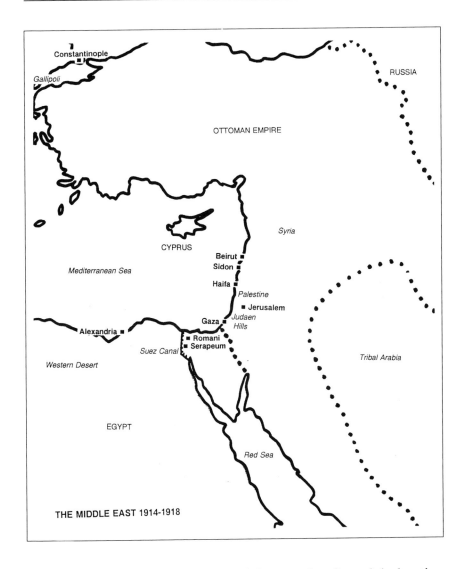

Constantinople
Gallipoli
RUSSIA
OTTOMAN EMPIRE
Syria
CYPRUS
Beirut
Sidon
Mediterranean Sea
Haifa
Palestine
Jerusalem
Judaen
Hills
Gaza
Alexandria
Romani
Serapeum
Suez Canal
Western Desert
Tribal Arabia
EGYPT
Red Sea
THE MIDDLE EAST 1914-1918

that a surprise attack on the canal might precede a formal declaration of war. German and Turkish agents had for some time been active in Egypt and Sudan seeking to discredit the British. In fact, Turkey declared war in November 1914 but did not move against the canal until February 1915, when a force of at least twelve thousand Turks was successfully driven off near Serapeum, largely by Indian troops, and 'A' Squadron joined battle to harass the Turkish retreat. More than sixteen hundred prisoners were taken.

'A' Squadron was to serve for four years in the Middle East. In May 1915 the bulk of the 42nd Division joined the Allied attempt to march

Turkish prisoners. More than sixteen hundred Turks were taken prisoner during the battle for the Suez Canal.

on Constantinople through landings on the Gallipoli peninsula. 'A' Squadron did not join this ill-fated venture, but sent a detachment for garrison duty at Cyprus, to release infantry for the campaign, while later in the year they fought in the Western Desert against the Senussi, an Islamic religious sect with followers in Egypt, Sudan and Arabia, that the Turks and Germans had persuaded to invade Egypt. The campaign was successful, with the capture of several Senussi leaders.

1916 saw a renewed threat to the Suez Canal. Turkish confidence was high after the failure of the Gallipoli venture, which the Allies finally abandoned, evacuating the peninsula, in January 1916. In July 1916 the Turks moved against the canal with about eighteen thousand men, but a battle at Romani in the northern Sinai Desert left the Turkish army again in retreat.

The follow up to this and other successes was, however, to be long delayed. The Middle East had a low priority for military resources once the Suez Canal was secured – indeed in March 1917 the 42nd Division was called to France, where there was a more desperate need. However, 'A' Squadron, now expert at desert reconnaissance, stayed in the Middle East, and by October 1917 forces were organised for a large scale advance under General Allenby.

'A' Squadron was linked with 'A' and 'B' Squadron of the Hertfordshire Yeomanry to form the 21st Corps Composite Cavalry Regiment. Gaza was captured on November 7th 1917 and a rapid advance into the Judaen Hills followed, trench warfare giving way to open warfare and then hill fighting. For weeks 'A' Squadron faced

DLOY on patrol in the Judean Hills (now the occupied West Bank).

extremes of heat and cold, riding over dusty plains and in harsh stony hills, often on short rations. There were casualties from both skirmishing and disease, but the momentum of the advance was never lost. Early in December Jerusalem was entered. Only then was a halt called.

Supply line problems, particularly of water, delayed further advance for some months. Finally, in September 1918, another general offensive was launched. At spectacular speed the 21st Corps Cavalry moved north, through Haifa, Acre, Tyre, Sidon and Beirut, to enter Tripoli on 13 October. When on 31 October 1918 an armistice with Turkey was announced, 'A' Squadron were at Khan Abdi, just north of Tripoli, many suffering from malaria and dysentery. They had fought and ridden over four hundred miles in little over a month. After several days' rest the squadron returned to Beirut to make a more permanent camp in time for Christmas.

In Palestine Allenby had conducted one of the most successful campaigns in history – and that victory owed much to the mounted forces. Over 75,000 prisoners had been taken in the final advance. British battle casualties were just over five thousand killed, wounded and missing. It was the last time that mounted forces were to play both a major and a successful role in war.

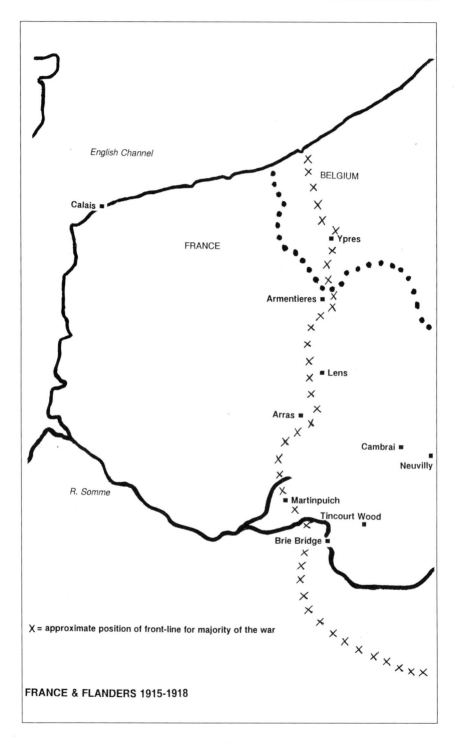

English Channel

BELGIUM

Calais ■

FRANCE

■ Ypres

Armentieres ■

■ Lens

Arras ■

Cambrai ■

■
Neuvilly

R. Somme

■ Martinpuich

Tincourt Wood
■

Brie Bridge ■

X = approximate position of front-line for majority of the war

FRANCE & FLANDERS 1915-1918

France and Flanders

During the latter half of 1915 and the early part of 1916, 'C' and 'D' Squadrons spent long periods dismounted and in the trenches alongside the infantry. 'C' Squadron, having landed at Le Havre on August 28 1915, served with the 23rd Division near Armentieres and Lens, in France, while 'D' Squadron saw its baptism of fire near Ypres, just inside Belgium, with the 14th (Light) Division.

The squadrons rarely served complete – instead sections were allotted to a variety of tasks. The particular speciality of the yeomanry, their ability as scouts to observe, record and report accurately, led some to work in observation posts, reporting on newly-dug German trenches and gun positions. Individuals also gained reputations as marksmen, and became specialist snipers. Men in both squadrons did their share of manhandling supplies, guarding prisoners, preparing further lines of defence, and burying the dead, in addition to providing infantry reinforcements. But throughout the DLOY kept their horses, albeit well behind the lines, and used them on occasion in work as divisional guides, controlling traffic at crossroads, and in guarding key points.

In 1916 divisional cavalry squadrons were formed into larger units, attached to army corps rather than divisions. 'C' and 'D' Squadrons of the DLOY were united and linked with 'A' Squadron of the Surrey Yeomanry to form the 3rd Corps Composite Cavalry Regiment. The General Staff expected the Somme offensive (July–November 1916) to end the static trench warfare and wanted a mounted force readily available to each corps to exploit quickly any breakthrough into the unbroken country behind the German lines. The offensive failed and the 3rd Corps Cavalry were soon back reinforcing the infantry in the sniper and observation post role. From one post near Martinpuich in September 1916 an officer of the DLOY witnessed the first attack using tanks.

In March 1917 the Germans completed a new line of defences behind their existing trench system on the Western Front. It was known as the 'Hindenberg Line', after the Chief of the German General Staff. As the Germans retired to these prepared positions the cavalry were briefly used in the mounted role to harass them. The 3rd Corps Cavalry saw action near Brie Bridge and Tincourt Wood, but static warfare soon returned and they entered the trenches yet again.

Later in 1917 the 3rd Corps Cavalry Regiment was disbanded, its members finally becoming full-time infantry, many in the 12th Battalion, The Manchester Regiment. In this designation men formerly of the DLOY saw some of the most desperate fighting of the war.

Mounted DLOY passing through a devastated landscape near Brie Bridge in France, March 1917.

During the German spring offensive (March–May 1918) the 12th Battalion suffered 27 killed, 102 wounded and 108 missing in just one day's hand-to-hand fighting near Rocquigny. Later, in October, during the final Allied offensive of the war, a battle at Neuvilly reduced the battalion of over eight hundred men to four officers and three hundred other ranks. It was a savage period of war, with little mercy shown on either side until an Armistice was declared on 11 November, 1918.

One striking example of a former yeomanry man serving as infantry concerns Henry Ware, who in fact joined the 23rd Battalion, The Manchester Regiment. His posthumous citation for the award of a Distinguished Conduct Medal is particularly evocative of the horror and heroism of the First World War:

For conspicuous gallantry and devotion to duty during a raid on the enemy's trenches. He pushed ahead of the raiding party and started to cut the wire in face of heavy rifle fire and bursting bombs. He was severely wounded, but, flinging himself across the wire, continued to cut it. When the rest of the party reached him he held down the uncut wire and ordered the men to walk over him. Throughout he showed the greatest fortitude, and his self-sacrifice undoubtedly enabled the others to reach the enemy trench.[29]

Ireland

*D*uring the war new units were raised that also wore the DLOY badge. These were second and third line battalions, known as the 2/1st and 3/1st DLOY. The 2/1st fulfilled the Territorial's traditional home defence role now that the first line was serving abroad, while the 3/1st served as a recruiting and training unit for the first and second line battalions. Ironically, however, it was the 3/1st that saw some action, when it was based at the Curragh in Ireland, at the time of the Easter uprising of 1916. No details are known of the Regiment's role, but one officer at least of the 3/1st DLOY was recorded in *The Times* as being wounded.[30]

Chapter Seven

Between the Wars
1919–1939

Last Minute Reprieve

Throughout 1919 and 1920 the Duke of Lancaster's Own Yeomanry existed virtually in name only, and awaited its fate. Post-war reforms of the yeomanry and regular cavalry forces were expected to be sweeping and the official loss of 'mounted' status was feared. It was thought significant that as 'A' Squadron returned from the Middle East most of their riding equipment was ordered to be handed into store in Beirut. Once in England the Squadron was paid off. The same fate awaited men formerly of 'C' and 'D' Squadrons who had served latterly as infantry.

In March 1921 the fears seemed confirmed when orders were received to re-form as a field artillery regiment. Enlistment for this very different training began, but two months later the orders were reversed – the DLOY was to revert to being mounted cavalry. It was a rare exception to the 1921 re-organisation and owed much to the fact that Lord Derby was Minister of War at the time. As finally re-formed the Regiment had three squadrons, with Regimental Headquarters retained at Whalley Range and a detached Machine-Gun Troop at Liverpool.

AC Squadron:	Manchester
B Squadron:	Bolton and Rainhill
D Squadron:	Blackpool and Preston

The Lancashire Hussars were not so lucky, as their conversion to artillery was determined upon. However, all who wished to stay with a mounted unit were permitted to join the DLOY with no loss of seniority.[31]

Annual Camps Continue

B *etween* 1922 and 1938 the annual camps continued, when for a fortnight the Regiment again trained for the divisional cavalry role with other territorial units.[32] Treasury funds might now provide the horses, but they were never generous – for example at one time recruits were allocated only ten rounds of ammunition per year on which to learn to shoot. Officers often personally financed this and other shortfalls. Recruitment to the Regiment was boosted in April 1939 when, in the aftermath of the Munich crisis, military conscription in peacetime was introduced. This was the first time this had occurred in British history. Membership of the Territorial Army exempted men from this compulsory military service since they already undertook voluntary military training and would be embodied for full-time service immediately war broke out. Many young men joined TA units, which were also expanded at this time, in preference to running the risk of drafting to unknown and unwanted units.

A Famous Volunteer

O *ne recruit* admitted to the ranks as a humble trooper just before the war was Arthur Lowe, years later to become famed for his portrayal of 'Captain Mainwaring' in the BBC TV comedy series on the Home Guard, *Dad's Army*.[33]

The Territorial Force had been re-styled in the aftermath of the First World War as the 'Territorial Army for Imperial Defence'. Every volunteer now had to accept liability for service anywhere overseas; thus when the Second World War broke out on 3 September 1939, the Regiment was prepared for service wherever required.

Chapter Eight

The Second World War

Introduction

*T**he* Regiment received its orders to mobilise on 1 September 1939, and concentrated in the Ramsbottom area. The mobilised strength was 32 officers, eight warrant officers, one staff sergeant, 34 sergeants, 583 rank and file. Cavalry training continued, with much time also spent on the ranges and in signals training.

However, by the end of October shocking (but hardly unexpected) news had reached the Regiment – all the pre-war training was to be overturned, the horses were to embark for Palestine, but the men were to stay in the United Kingdom for equipping and training as artillery. Two Medium Regiments, Royal Artillery, were eventually formed from the existing Regiment.[34]

Training naturally changed abruptly to include driving instruction, vehicle maintenance and gunnery. Conscripts were drafted into the

4th (Blackpool) Troop, 'D' Squadron, in November 1939. This photograph was taken only days after the conversion of the Regiment to artillery was announced.

Army Form E.518

RESERVE AND AUXILIARY FORCES ACT, 1939.
TERRITORIAL ARMY.

CALLING OUT NOTICE.

To—

Name ....Norman A.V...

Rank.............L/SJT.. Army Number 97973......

Regt. or Corps.........D.L. OYEOMANRY...

    In pursuance of directions given by the Secretary of State for War in accordance with an Order in Council made under Section 1 of the above-mentioned Act, you are hereby notified that you are called out for military service commencing from

1 SEP 1939   19 , and for this purpose you are required to join the

....

at...........BOLTON..on that day.

    Should you not present yourself on that day you will be liable to be proceeded against.

Stamp of Officer Commanding Unit.

BOLTON.

Place..

Date ....1 SEP 1939.......................

    You should bring your Health and Pensions Insurance Card and Unemployment Insurance Book. If, however, you cannot obtain these before joining you should write to your employer asking him to forward these to you at your unit headquarters. If you are in possession of a receipt (U.I. 40) from the Employment Exchange for your Employment Book bring that receipt with you.
    You will also bring your Army Book 3, but you must not fill in any particulars on page 13 or the " Statement of family " in that book, and the postcards therein must not be used.

[5/39] (393/2397) Wt. 21114 750M 7/39 H & S Ltd. Gp. 393 (2242) Forms E518/1

DLOY call-out notice dated 1 September 1939. On this day, two days before the actual declaration of war, the Territorial Army was mobilised.

---

regiments and many of the pre-war volunteers left to join other units,[35] but a hard core successfully made the conversion to artillery, and the yeomanry foundation was certainly not forgotten – the new units were officially titled the 77th and 78th (DLOY) Medium Regiments, Royal Artillery. Their members wore DLOY collar and shoulder badges throughout the war and DLOY cap badges for as long as existing stocks lasted. More poignantly their war dead were ultimately to be buried under headstones carrying the yeomanry and

On ration fatigue at Rawtenstall, January 1940. The recruitment posters in the background appear somewhat ironic – 'Join the Modern Army'!

not the artillery badge. The new regiments were in place by April 1940, the 77th at Pembroke Dock, where they saw early action as witnesses to Luftwaffe air raids, in the course of which one man was fatally wounded; the first DLOY casualty of this second world war.

78th (DLOY) Medium Regiment, Royal Artillery 1940–1946

Finally to War

*I*n January 1943 the 78th sailed from Liverpool for the Middle East, where months of further training in Palestine, Syria and Egypt proved useful if tedious. Finally, in November, orders were received to embark for Taranto in Italy. The 78th joined the eastern flank of the Italian front in the River Sangro area, and on 9 January 1944 the guns were fired in anger for the first time.

Action at Cassino

*I*n April 1944 the 78th were ordered to the western flank, to support a renewed assault on Monastery Hill at Cassino. The German defence of Cassino was one of the most effective rearguard actions of the Second World War. The Allies were advancing north through Italy towards Rome, the capture of which would give an obvious boost to Allied morale. To delay this as long as possible the heavily outnumbered Germans organised a defence line, known as the 'Gustav Line', in the hills south of Rome.

Nature favoured the defenders. The River Rapido formed a barrier to all, while parts of the valley were too marshy for a tank attack. The town of Cassino was less important than the hill with its monastery that rose behind it. On this hill, overlooking both town and river, the German 1st Parachute Division, some of Germany's toughest troops, were dug in.

Three Allied attacks against Monastery Hill had already failed when the 78th (DLOY) Medium Regiment moved to the area. On 11 May 1944 a further assault began, the 78th supporting in the first instance the British 10th Infantry Brigade, who attacked across the Rapido in inflatable assault craft and established a bridgehead.

The fighting was extremely fierce. The artillery of each side duelled and one gun of the 78th received a direct hit, killing nine men. The position remained critical for several days, until a French push to the south of Cassino broke the Gustav Line and forced the Germans to retreat for fear of being outflanked. The monastery, long since a heap of rubble, was finally occupied by Polish soldiers, supported by the fire of the 78th. Less than three weeks later the Allies entered Rome. Between 11 and 25 May, in their first major engagement, the 78th's 5.5 inch guns fired over 22,000 shells.

A crew from the 78th Medium Regiment posing by their 5.5″ gun, near San Eusanio, Italy in January 1944.

By the winter of 1944 the 78th were within thirty miles of Bologna, with high hopes of a rapid advance to the Alps. However, the mud of the Lombardy Plain and the diversion of resources to the front in North West Europe caused a halt near the River Senio.

The spring of 1945 saw a renewed push which included New Zealand, Gurkha and Polish units. Enemy resistance now collapsed. The River Po was crossed at Ferrara, followed by the River Adige, where the 78th fired their last rounds of the war.

On Horseback Again

*W*ith the end of hostilities the 78th moved to Trieste where, remarkably, one squadron briefly became mounted again, serving as auxiliary mounted policemen in the Venetia Guilia Police. This force, raised as a combination of British soldiers and Italians but gradually increasing over a two-year period to 100% Italian personnel, did valuable work in calming the riotous streets of Trieste, and also in patrolling the sensitive Italian–Yugoslavian border.

77th (DLOY) Medium Regiment, Royal Artillery 1940–1946

Landing in Normandy

*T*he 77th trained in the United Kingdom until 1944, when on 'D-Day + 9' (15 June) the Regiment disembarked on 'M' Beach. It was cold and wet, with gunfire audible in the distance, but there was no direct enemy interference. Next day the guns were in place ready for action near Lantheuil, in support of the 3rd Canadian Division.

The fighting in Normandy was fierce. The German defenders found excellent cover in a region noted for its sunken lanes and thick hedgerows, and the 77th faced the constant threat of snipers in addition to the probing of German artillery in counter-battery shoots. Near the end of June the 77th provided close supporting fire for the 15th (Scottish) Division during 'Operation Epsom', the first major attempt by the British to break out from the Normandy bridgehead.

'Operation Goodwood' followed in mid-July, with support provided for the 7th, 11th and Guards Armoured Divisions, but it was not until early in August, after 'Operation Bluecoat', that the British were able to push forward with any momentum. Even then the Germans continued to prove adept at a system of pocket defence based on a

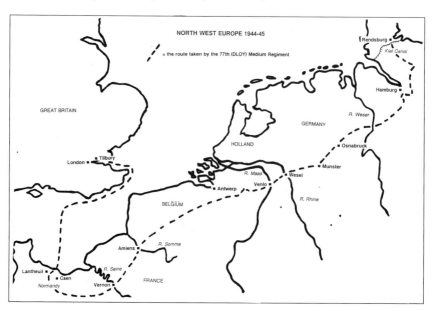

64

single tank, a section of infantry and a couple of engineers skilled in booby-trapping. Still, tactics of 'batter through or by-pass' meant that by 18 September the 77th were poised to enter Belgium and Holland with the 3rd and 15th (Scottish) Divisions.

In Holland progress was slow. Large areas were deliberately flooded by the retreating Germans, while heavy rain added to the problem; gun positions repeatedly filled with water. Meanwhile, the main Allied thrust was towards Germany, and in March 1945 the 77th moved to support this.

Into Germany – The Rhine Crossing

*T*he Regiment crossed the River Maas and entered Germany. Ahead lay the River Rhine. To support the crossing of the Rhine, which was the last major obstacle facing the Western Allies in their advance into Germany, practically every gun on the Western Front was brought up – including those of the 77th. On the evening of 23 March the guns supported a crossing of the Rhine by the 1st Commando Brigade, who formed a bridgehead near Wesel. The next morning it was planned to make further landings, this time from the air. The problem lay in getting the planes and gliders carrying the airborne troops past the defending German guns. This led to one of the biggest counter-battery programmes ever devised. It had to be effective in knocking out these guns just before the attack, since while the seventeen hundred planes and thirteen hundred gliders were over the target (a period of about three hours) no heavy artillery fire could continue for fear of the shells hitting the aircraft.

It was decided to use two observers, one back from the river to note the incoming planes and one overlooking the dropping area. With this method the guns could be kept firing to the last moment, instead of having to keep to a timed programme which, should the aircraft be late, would leave the German gunners time to collect their wits.

At 9.30am on 24 March 1945 the barrage commenced. It lasted 22 minutes, until the first aircraft was near the target. It was not a long enough time in which to locate and destroy every gun in a target area ten miles wide by six across. For almost three hours the gunners were then silent, those near the river forced to watch grimly as the Germans recovered and put up a fierce resistance.

The British 6th Airborne Division suffered heavily, almost half its gliders being shot down or damaged in the air. The American 17th Airborne Division was more fortunate in its initial assault, though the second wave took heavy casualties. Fortunately, once on the ground, the airborne force (albeit depleted) was able to be supported by the guns again, and a link-up with the infantry in the Wesel bridgehead was achieved. The battle was won.

Thereafter the advance was rapid – Dorsten, Dulmen, Buldern, Munster and Osnabruck, where a chaotic situation diverted the 77th for a time. Large numbers of released slave workers, many from the Soviet Union, roamed the area, all needing to be sent to rearward areas in the unit transport. Thousands of German prisoners also required guarding, feeding and transporting.

Post-War Duties

*W*hen the German surrender was announced in May 1945 the 77th were poised to support an assault on Hamburg by the 15th (Scottish) Division. They moved to occupy Eider barracks at Rendsburg on the Kiel Canal, and for the rest of the year policed the area. Tasks included controlling the Kiel Canal Barrier, rounding up remnants of the German forces, identifying those suspected of war crimes, evacuating former slave workers, and patrolling generally to enforce law and order.

Chapter Nine

Post-War Years
1947–Present Day

*A**fter* the Second World War more re-organisation led to a drastic change in the 'Duke's Own'. No more artillery but also no return to horses – instead the decision to become a tank regiment, the Royal Armoured Corps being the modern successors to the cavalry. The DLOY were affiliated as a TA unit to the regular 14th/20th (King's) Hussars, a unit which had fought alongside the 78th in Italy, and which was now allocated Lancashire as its recruiting area.

Cromwell tank of the DLOY on display in Manchester during a recruiting drive, circa 1949.

In 1956 the Regiment's role changed to that of a Home Defence Reconnaissance Regiment of the Royal Armoured Corps. Equipped with Land Rovers and armoured cars, the Regiment's wartime task was to locate, track and report on enemy units.

On 24 May 1961 the Regiment received a new Guidon from the Colonel-in-Chief, Her Majesty Queen Elizabeth II, and a march past in vehicles was held. The old Guidon was laid up in Manchester Cathedral.

The late 1960s saw a great reduction in the Territorial Army and by April 1969 the DLOY found themselves reduced to a cadre of eight all ranks. A Lancashire territorial unit of the Royal Engineers briefly adopted the yeomanry title, to become 202nd (DLOY) Field Squadron, Royal Engineers, but this was to be a short-lived arrangement. In April 1971 the Regiment was re-formed, now in an Infantry Home Defence Role, with the Regimental Headquarters ('Lancaster House') re-located to Chorley in 1982.

In 1983 the rôle of the DLOY again reverted to that of a Home Defence Reconnaissance Regiment, equipped with Land Rovers. The Regiment remained part of the Royal Armoured Corps, drawing

The DLOY photographed at West Down Camp, as infantry, in 1976.

HM the Queen presenting the DLOY with their third Guidon, at Stonyhurst, Lancashire in 1990. The painting was commissioned by the Regiment.

permanent-staff instructors from it, and the regular army affiliation was still to the 14th/20th (King's) Hussars.

In 1984 the Regimental Museum, a recent creation housed initially in a room at Rufford Old Hall, was re-located to the Lancashire County and Regimental Museum at Preston, itself a new development. Neighbouring galleries, appropriately enough, soon housed (amongst others) the regimental museum of the 14th/20th (King's) Hussars.

Throughout the 1980s the Regimental Headquarters remained at Chorley, with squadron centres at Wigan ('A' Squadron), Clifton ('B'), Chorley ('C' – Home Service Force) and Preston/Blackpool ('D').

This organisation is, however, soon to change. Late in 1991 the Regiment learned that as part of the major review of the armed services that followed the disintegration of the Warsaw Pact, the DLOY was to be drastically reduced. From mid-1992 it will form but a single squadron within a 'new' Yeomanry regiment, after amalgamating with the Queen's Own Mercian Yeomanry. 'D' (Duke of Lancaster's Own) Squadron will be based at Kearsley House in

Wigan, 'A' Squadron DLOY's former home.

DLOY insignia, excepting only the cap badge, will be retained by the squadron who will, no doubt, also strive to maintain many traditions from their proud regimental past. The annual duty to provide a dismounted guard for the trophies at the Grand National winners' enclosure at Aintree will hopefully survive; each year this gains coverage on national television and gives us all the chance to admire the full dress uniform of the Duke of Lancaster's Own Yeomanry, and thereby be reminded of this historic Lancastrian Regiment.

Notes

1. A sabre, believed to be from this unit and decorated with a 'liver bird' on the blade, is displayed in the DLOY Museum.
2. A copy of an illustration of Captain Farington (also written as ffarington), one-time commanding officer of the Preston and Chorley Light Horse, is displayed in the DLOY Museum.
3. Although many urban middle-class tradesmen also owned horses and formed a significant proportion of the volunteers in some units, especially in Lancashire – see note 8.
4. The original 1805 muster roll can be seen in the DLOY Museum.
5. For example, in 1834 Liverpool had a population of 250,000 but only fifty night watchmen. Improvements followed the 1835 Municipal Corporations Act, which encouraged towns and boroughs to set up police forces, but progress was slow. Co-operation between forces was also very limited, and it was not until late in the century that the police could raise sufficient numbers, even in the big cities, effectively to subdue mass disturbances unaided by the military. If warning was given of trouble the magistrates might enrol temporary special constables (see Chapter Two) but these were not wholly reliable, especially in disputes with political overtones.
6. Quoted from a secondary source in DLOY archives – no reference given.
7. Wheeler's *Manchester Chronicle*, 29 April 1826, referring to riots that occurred at Low Moor, Clitheroe on 25 April 1826.
8. A list was given in *Wooler's British Gazette and Manchester Observer*, 10 August 1822, of the 101 members of the Manchester and Salford Yeomanry present at Peterloo. Their occupations were given as follows:

Cotton manufacturers 7
Cotton merchants 7
Calico printers 3
Warehousemen 3
Dyers 2
Drysalter 1
Publicans 13
Brewer 1
Brewer's clerk 1
Wine merchant 1
Butchers 7
Cheesemongers 2
Butter factor 1
Corn dealer 1
Flour dealer 1
Iron-liquor merchants 2
Paper maker 1
Servant 1
Saddlers 2
Coachmaker 1
Horse-breaker 1
Farrier 1
Stable keeper 1
Coachman 1
Hackney writer 1
Ironmongers 2
Tobacconists 2
Shopkeeper 1
Watchmakers 2
Tailor 1
Plumber 1
Painter 1
Attornies 3
Surgeons 2
Quack doctor 1
Labourer 1
Insurance agent 1
Dancing master 1

Twenty-one members were listed without occupations. The high number of publicans among the volunteers is easily explained; it was noted at the time how this group was anxious to curry favour with the magistracy since, of course, they required their licences renewing annually. Certainly in Bolton in 1842 one publican was refused a renewal of a licence because, barely a week before, he had failed to turn out as a special constable during rioting.

9. From an account by the Rev Edward Stanley, Rector of Alderley, quoted in D. Read, *Peterloo - The 'Massacre' and its Background* (Manchester, 1958).

10. Ibid.

11. A presentation sabre was given to one of the defendants in rather tactless celebration of his acquittal, and can be seen in the DLOY Museum. The defendant was Major Birley, who held the rank of captain at Peterloo. In 1820 he was promoted to major and was commanding officer of the unit at the time of the trial.

12. Occasionally the full toast, 'The Queen, Duke of Lancaster' is used, but the shorter version is commonly employed in the Regiment.

13. All the following quotations are from either the *Bolton Free Press* or the *Bolton Chronicle* for 13 August 1842, 20 August 1842 and 27 August 1842.

14. The police office was in Bowker's Row, off Nelson Square.

15. Captain Langshaw, the troop commander, was 'absent from England', hence Fletcher's role. John Fletcher was, in addition, a magistrate, and had been involved in countering similar riots in Bolton in 1839. He was the son of 'Colonel' Ralph Fletcher, who had suppressed the 'Luddite' riots in 1812 at Westhoughton.

16. The insult 'cabbage cutters' was apparently widely used, perhaps even nationally, against the yeomanry. This has sometimes been thought to refer to the agricultural background of many of the yeomanry (they might have been regarded as yokels by the urban crowds), but in fact it refers more directly to their training - at this date they practised swordhandling on horseback by slashing at cabbages.

17. An example of an officer's complete full dress uniform, dating from the 1850s, can be seen in the DLOY Museum. The same family had raised the Ashton Cavalry back in 1789.

18. A reference in the *Bolton Chronicle* of 21 October 1876 to the funeral of an old soldier states that with the regiment he had attended 'sundry election riots' but it is not clear what period is being referred to. Another incident of interest is the use in 1846 of the Westmorland and Cumberland Yeomanry to prevent pitched battles between English and Irish navvies building the Carlisle to Lancaster railway near Penrith. One wonders if there were similar incidents in Lancashire!

19. An account of the day, with illustrations showing the DLOY, appeared in the *Illustrated London News* of 11 July 1857.

20. By 1914 the Blackburn Troop had moved to Preston, to a drill hall on Hartington Road.

21. The *Lancaster Gazette* of 25 June 1864 contains an account of a typical annual camp and inspection. One exception to Lancaster was the year 1872, when training took place in Preston because it was rumoured that there was an epidemic of smallpox and fever in Lancaster.

22. See the *Bolton Chronicle*, 21 October 1876, p7.

23. An account of the presentation, which took place during the annual camp of 1877, appears in the *Lancaster Guardian*, 30 June 1877, p8. The sword is on display in the DLOY Museum. The longest-lived survivor of the Charge of the Light Brigade was one Edwin Hughes, who died in Blackpool in 1927, 73 years after the Charge!

24. A re-created scene of the Liverpool

dockside on this day can be seen in the DLOY Museum.

25. The *Afric* saw further service as a troop-transport in the 1914–18 war, bringing Australian volunteers to Europe. She was torpedoed and sunk off the Eddystone on 12 February 1917, with the loss of five lives.

26. A detachment of 25 men under Captain L. G. S. Molloy went to London to line part of the processional route.

27. This event is recorded in *The Cheshire (Earl of Chester's) Yeomanry 1898-1967* by Lt. Col. Sir R. Verdin (1971), pp40-1.

28. The evidence for this dissection of 'B' Squadron is taken from the inscription on a piece of regimental silver, namely the model of a mounted trooper in First World War uniform, presented to the officers by Col. D. H. Bates, MC, TD, in 1934 and now held at Regimental Headquarters at Chorley. In Col. Bates' papers in the regimental archives he states simply that 'A' Squadron and 25 MMP went to Egypt.

29. *London Gazette* entry 26 January 1918, p1336. Cpl. Ware died of his wounds on 26 August 1917.

30. *The Times*, 29 April 1916, p10: 'Wounded . . . Lieut. H. H. Thompson D.L.O.Y.'. Harold Horner Thompson, born 1886, educated at Rossall, was a salt manufacturer from Northwich.

31. In 1925 Lt. Col. H. A. Bromilow, TD, formerly a major in the Lancashire Hussars, became CO of the DLOY.

32. A cine film of some inter-war camps is known to have existed. The museum would welcome knowledge of its current whereabouts.

33. Lowe may have joined in November 1938, this being the usual month for admitting new recruits to the Regiment at that time. He apparently served as a trooper in the stores at Regimental HQ, and after the outbreak of war stayed for the conversion to the 77th (Medium) Regiment, Royal Artillery. About 1943 he transferred to the Royal Engineers, eventually to reach the rank of Sergeant Major.

34. 'HQ' and 'AC' Squadrons formed the 77th; 'B' and 'D' Squadrons formed the 78th.

35. A significant number seem to have left for Officer Training Units.

Bibliography

Anglesey, G. C. H. V. P., 7th Marquess of, *A History of the British Cavalry 1816–1919. Vol. 1: 1816–1850; Vol. 2: 1851–1871; Vol. 3: 1872–1898; Vol. 4: 1899–1913* (Leo Cooper, 1973, 1975, 1982, 1986).

Barlow, L., and Smith, R. J., *The Uniforms of the British Yeomanry Force 1794–1914: Vol. 6: The Duke of Lancaster's Own Yeomanry* (Robert Ogilby Trust, 1983).

Bastick, Lt. Col. J. D., *Trumpet Call – The Story of the Duke of Lancaster's Own Yeomanry* (published by the Regiment, 1973).

Earle, T. A., *List of Officers who have served in the Lancashire Hussars Yeomanry Cavalry; with some short notes and annals of the Regiment since its formation in 1848 to the present time* (1889).

Fell, A., *A Furness Military Chronicle*, especially chapter viii on the Furness Troop of Yeomanry Cavalry (Kitchin & Co., 1937).

Gibbon, F. P., *The 42nd (East Lancashire Division) 1914–1918* (Country Life, 1920).

Johnson, Trooper L. H., *The Duke of Lancaster's Own Yeomanry Cavalry, 23rd Company, Imperial Yeomanry* (published by the author, 1902).

Mileham, P. J. R., *The Yeomanry Regiments – A Pictorial History* (Spellmount Ltd., 1985).

Read, D., *Peterloo – The 'Massacre' and its Background* (Manchester University Press, 1958).

Thomas, L. J., *The 77th (D.L.O.Y.) Medium Regiment, R.A. – North West Europe Campaign, June 1944–May 1945* (published by the Regiment(?), c.1946).